Edison ES

Montana
Facts and Symbols

by Shelley Swanson Sateren

Consultant:
Mary Boyle, Publicity Coordinator
Travel Montana

Capstone press
Mankato, Minnesota

Capstone Press
151 Good Counsel Drive, P.O. Box 669, Mankato, Minnesota 56002
http://www.capstone-press.com

Library of Congress Cataloging-in-Publication Data
Sateren, Shelley Swanson
    Montana facts and symbols/by Shelley Swanson Sateren—Rev. and updated ed.
    p. cm.—(The states and their symbols)
    Includes bibliographical references (p. 23) and index.
    Summary: Presents information about the state of Montana, its nickname, motto,
and emblems.
    ISBN 0-7368-2256-9 (hardcover)
    1. Emblems, State—Montana—Juvenile literature. [1. Emblems, State—Montana.
2. Montana.] I. Title. II. Series.
CR203.M9S28 2003
978.6—dc21   2002154837

Editorial Credits

Christianne C. Jones, update editor; Christy Steele, editor; Linda Clavel update
    designer and illustrator; Heather Kindseth, cover designer; Jo Miller, update photo
    researcher; Kimberly Danger, photo researcher

Photo Credits

George Robbins Photo, cover
Index Stock Imagery/R. Helfrick, 6
Joe McDonald, 12
John Elk III, 10, 22 (top)
Lynn Gerig, 22 (middle)/Tom Stack and Associates
One Mile Up, Inc., 8, 10 (inset)
Photo Network/Mark Newman, 18
Unicorn Stock Photos/David P. Dill, 20
Visuals Unlimited/Richard Thom, 14; Gerald Corsi, 16
William Muñoz, 22 (bottom)

1 2 3 4 5 6 08 07 06 05 04 03

Table of Contents

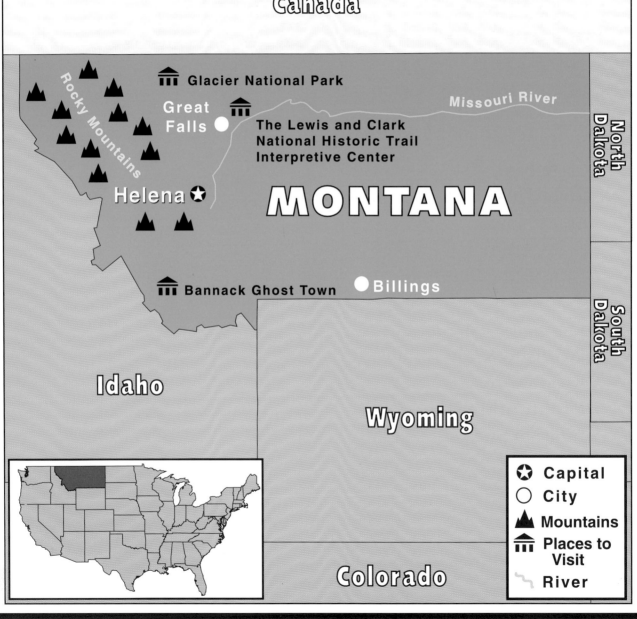

Canada

Rocky Mountains

🏛 Glacier National Park

Great
Falls ●

🏛 The Lewis and Clark
National Historic Trail
Interpretive Center

Missouri River

North Dakota

Helena ⭐

MONTANA

🏛 Bannack Ghost Town ● Billings

South Dakota

Idaho

Wyoming

Colorado

⭐ Capital
◯ City
⛰ Mountains
🏛 Places to Visit
〰 River

Fast Facts

Capital: Helena is Montana's capital.

Largest City: Billings is Montana's largest city. Almost 90,000 people live in Billings.

Size: Montana covers 147,046 square miles (380,849 square kilometers). Montana is the 4th largest state.

Location: Montana is in the northwestern United States.

Population: 902,195 people live in Montana (2000 U.S. Census Bureau).

Statehood: Montana became the 41st state on November 8, 1889.

Natural Resources: Montanans mine copper, gold, and zinc. Workers harvest wood from Montana's forests.

Manufactured Goods: Montanans make food products, wood products, and paper products.

Crops: Montana farmers grow wheat, barley, and sugar beets. Livestock farmers raise cattle, sheep, and hogs.

State Name and Nickname

The name Montana comes from a Latin word that means mountainous. Mountains and valleys cover the western half of Montana. The mountains are part of the Rocky Mountains. Plains lie in the eastern half of the state.

Montana's official nickname shows the importance of mining in the state. The Treasure State nickname stands for Montana's valuable metals such as gold. Many settlers moved to Montana to look for gold and silver.

Two of Montana's nicknames come from its landscape. Big Sky Country is Montana's most famous nickname. From Montana's plains, the sky looks like a huge blue roof. Few large buildings exist to block the open view. The nickname Land of Shining Mountains refers to Montana's many snow-covered mountains.

Mountains cover large parts of Montana. This landscape inspired the nickname of Land of Shining Mountains.

State Seal and Motto

Montana officials adopted the state seal in 1893. The seal reminds Montanans of their state's government. The seal also makes government papers official.

Montana's state seal represents the state's economy, landscape, and history. A plow, a shovel, and a pick stand for farming and mining. The sun rising over mountain peaks highlights Montana's landscape. The Great Falls of the Missouri River is on the seal. In 1805, explorers Meriwether Lewis and William Clark became the first white explorers to see this series of five waterfalls.

Montana's state motto is "Oro y Plata" (OR-oh ee PLAH-tuh). These Spanish words mean gold and silver. The motto suggests money and wealth. People discovered gold and silver in Montana's mountains 140 years ago.

In 1893, the manager of a jewelry company in Helena, Montana, engraved the new seal for $20.

MONTANA

State Capitol and Flag

Montana's capitol building is in Helena. Helena is the capital of Montana. Government officials work in the capitol. They make the state's laws there.

Workers built the capitol between 1899 and 1902. They used sandstone mined in Montana. A copper dome sits on top of the capitol. A statue of the Goddess of Liberty is on top of the dome. Over the years, builders have added east and west wings. Officials needed more room as the government grew.

Montana's flag began as a banner made for the First Montanan Infantry in 1898. Montana soldiers carried this cloth into battle. They fought Spanish soldiers in the Spanish-American War (1898).

Government officials adopted the banner as the state flag in 1905. Montana's state flag is blue. The state seal is in the center of the flag below the state name.

Montana's flag has had one major change since 1905. Officials added the state's name to the flag in 1981.

11

State Bird

Montana schoolchildren voted for the western meadowlark as Montana's state bird. The government made the schoolchildren's choice official in 1931.

An adult meadowlark is easy to spot. The bird is about 9 inches (23 centimeters) long. It has a bright yellow breast and black V-shaped spots on its throat.

Western meadowlarks can sing more than 200 notes a minute. Some notes sound steady like a whistle. Some notes sound like trills made on a flute. Birds quickly change between two notes to make trills.

Meadowlarks fly in a certain way to save energy. First, they quickly beat their wings. Then they coast for as long as possible. Meadowlarks will beat their wings again just before they drop too low.

Famous explorers Lewis and Clark first wrote about the western meadowlark in Montana in 1805.

State Tree

In 1908, Montana schoolchildren voted that the ponderosa pine best represented the state. Ponderosa pines grow throughout most of western Montana. Officials made the schoolchildren's choice official in 1949.

Ponderosa pines are evergreen trees. Their long, dark green needles stay green all year. Ponderosa pines grow red-brown cones. The cones hold the pine tree's seeds.

Ponderosa pines can live for 150 years. They grow 60 to 125 feet (18 to 38 meters) tall. Young trees have brown or black bark. Older trees have yellow-brown bark.

The ponderosa pine is a valuable wood. Settlers made railroad ties, telegraph poles, and houses from the strong wood. Selling ponderosa pine is a successful Montanan business. Sales of the wood total several million dollars each year.

Today, people use boards from ponderosa pines to make furniture and build houses.

State Flower

The bitterroot became Montana's state flower in 1895. The Montana Floral Emblem Association chose this wildflower. Bitterroot grows on Montana's hills and mountains.

The bitterroot has pleasant-smelling blossoms. The blossoms are about 2 inches (5 centimeters) across. Each blossom has about 16 petals. The petals are pink. The blossom's center is white and pink.

Bitterroots have almost no stem. The stems are about 2 inches (5 centimeters) tall. Bitterroots grow close to the ground for protection from cold winds.

Bitterroots were important to Montana's Native American people. Early Native Americans traded the plant's roots. A sack of the roots could buy a horse. Native Americans boiled the roots to take away the bitter taste. They then mixed the roots with meat or berries.

Bitterroots can live more than one year without water.

State Animal

In 1982, Montana schoolchildren voted for the state animal. They chose the grizzly bear. The grizzly bear became the official state animal in 1983. Montana has a large grizzly bear population.

Grizzlies are large bears. Adults grow to be 8 feet (2.4 meters) long. They weigh up to 1,000 pounds (454 kilograms).

Grizzly bears usually have brown fur. Each hair has a silver-colored tip. Grizzlies have short ears and a large, rounded hump on the neck. Their claws measure more than 2.5 inches (6 centimeters) long.

Grizzly bears use their strong sense of smell to find food. They eat mostly plants and fruits. Grizzlies can easily smell a plant bulb that is covered by dirt and snow. The bears use their long claws to dig for plant bulbs and roots.

Grizzly bears have a strong sense of smell. They can smell a person from 1 mile (1.6 kilometers) away.

More State Symbols

State Fish: Montana's governor named the blackspotted cutthroat trout the state fish in 1977. This fish is native to Montana. Fishers try to catch cutthroat trout in Montana's rivers and lakes.

State Fossil: *Maiasaura peeblesorum* became the state fossil in 1985. Scientists discovered the nests and eggs of this duck-billed dinosaur in Montana. The fossils on Montana's Egg Mountain have taught scientists a great deal about dinosaurs.

State Gemstones: Moss agates and sapphires have been the state gemstones since 1969. People make agates into jewelry. Montana's mines have produced more than $40 million worth of sapphires.

State Grass: Officials named bluebunch wheatgrass the state grass in 1973. This grass grows throughout Montana. Montana's cattle and sheep eat bluebunch wheatgrass. Livestock farming is one of Montana's major businesses.

Montanans made the cutthroat trout a state symbol because polluted water has put the fish in danger.

Places to Visit

Bannack Ghost Town

Bannack Ghost Town is in Bannack State Park. Montana's first major gold strike happened near Bannack in 1862. Everyone moved when the gold ran out. Many buildings in this town are still standing. Visitors explore the buildings in Bannack.

Glacier National Park

Glacier National Park is in northwestern Montana. Visitors to the park walk on large masses of slowly moving ice called glaciers. Glacier National Park has 700 miles (1,127 kilometers) of hiking trails. Visitors may see wild wolves, grizzly bears, mountain lions, and mountain goats.

Lewis and Clark Interpretive Center

The Lewis and Clark Interpretive Center is in the city of Great Falls. At the center, visitors watch a movie about explorers Lewis and Clark. From 1804 to 1806, they traveled 8,000 miles (12,874 kilometers) across the United States. Exhibits show the explorers' struggles and successes.

Words to Know

banner (BAN-ur)—a long piece of material with writing, pictures, or designs on it; people often display banners during important events.

explorer (ek-SPLOR-ur)—a person who travels to discover what a place is like

glacier (GLAY-shur)—a large mass of slowly moving ice

pick (PIK)—a tool with a sharp, metal bar on a long, wooden handle; people use picks to break up hard ground or rocks.

plain (PLANE)—a large area of land that is flat or nearly flat

Read More

Bennett, Clayton. *Montana.* Celebrate the States. New York: Benchmark Books, 2001.

Heinrichs, Ann. *Montana.* This Land Is Your Land. Minneapolis: Compass Point Books, 2003.

Kummer, Patricia K. *Montana.* One Nation. Mankato, Minn.: Capstone Press, 2003.

McLuskey, Krista. *Montana.* A Kid's Guide to American States. Mankato, Minn.: Weigl Publishers, 2002.

Useful Addresses

Montana Secretary of State
P.O. Box 202801
Helena, MT 59620-2801

Montana Travel Promotion Division
301 South Park Ave.
Helena, MT 59620-0133

Internet Sites

Do you want to find out more about Montana?
Let FactHound, our fact-finding hound dog, do the
research for you.

Here's how:
1) Visit **http://www.facthound.com**
2) Type in the **BOOK ID** number:
   0736822569
3) Click on **FETCH IT**.

FactHound will fetch Internet sites picked by
our editors just for you!

Index